Designing Music Environments for Early Childhood

MENC: The National Association for Music Education

Copyright © 2000
MENC: The National Association for Music Education
1806 Robert Fulton Drive, Reston, Virginia 20191
All Rights Reserved
Printed in the United States of America

ISBN: 978-1-56545-131-5

CONTENTS

Acknowledgements ii

Foreword. iii

1: The Music House 1

2: Going to the Ocean 4

3: Music on a Shoestring 10

4: Hickory Dickory Dock. 16

5: PVC Pipe Playstage 22

6: Tons of Drums 26

7: Mary Wore a Red Dress. 33

8: The Music Box. 39

9: What a Wonderful World. 48

ACKNOWLEDGMENTS

MENC gratefully acknowledges the compilers of this book:

Susan H. Kenney
Brigham Young University
Provo, Utah

Diane Persellin
Trinity University
San Antonio, Texas

MENC also gratefully acknowledges the following educators who contributed to this booklet:

Barbara Andress, Phoenix, Arizona

Lori Custodero, New York, New York

Sharla Dance, Redmond, Washington

Donna Brink Fox, Rochester, New York

Mary Ann Hall, Westport, Connecticut

Susan Kujawski, Litchfield Park, Arizona

Cecilia Riddell, Pasadena, California

Mark E. Turner, Austin, Texas

FOREWORD

Music experiences in early childhood create the very foundation upon which future music learning is built. Environments designed to encourage the young child to explore and play with musical sounds help make music learning a natural part of the child's world.

Places that invite children to become active participants in music play, allowing them to freely explore and interact at their own pace, with or without others, offer a rich combination of social, emotional, physical, and cognitive development opportunities. These places also help children to value their own music making.

This booklet is a compilation of methods, ideas, and suggestions for creating special places—music environments—to encourage music making by young children. Developed by early childhood music experts over years of experience and research, the suggestions here also offer ways to effectively explore the Prekindergarten Music Education Standards.

These ideas may be helpful to parents, as well as child care providers, head start teachers, and preschool educators who provide learning opportunities to the 15 million children under the age of five in child-care and preschool settings in the United States. We hope you find the ideas in this booklet useful, and that the ideas stimulate your own thinking to create other environments appropriate for your situation. Enjoy the musical play!

The Music House

APPROPRIATE AGES: 3-5 years

PREKINDERGARTEN MUSIC EDUCATION STANDARDS EXPLORED

Children will:

- Invent and use original graphic or symbolic systems to represent vocal and instrumental sounds and musical ideas
- Respond through movement to music of various tempos, meters, dynamics, modes, genres, and styles to express what they hear and feel in works of music

WHY THIS ENVIRONMENT?

This environment was based on what we've seen children enjoy doing on their own: building "forts" with blankets and furniture, and playing with flashlights.

We've added a musical component to an established favorite activity, believing that since children integrate music-making into their daily experiences, we should follow their lead when designing environments for them!

CREATED BY

Lori Custodero, Prof. of Music, and students from "Designing Musical Experiences for Young Children" at Teachers College, Columbia Univ. Music & Music Education Dept., Box 139/ 525 West 120th Street, New York, NY 10027

1: The Music House

PLAY MATERIALS
- High Table
- Two dark sheets
- Cassette tape recorder
- Flashlights
- Tape-looped recording of music such as Saint-Saens "The Swan" from *Carnival of the Animals*, and Haydn's *Symphony No. 94*, second movement

THE PLAY

Consider modeling this activity during circle time with a sheet on the wall. Teacher and/or individual children take turns "conducting" the music with flashlights. Opportunities exist for teachers to comment on what they see the child do in response to the music.

For example, describe the movements as fast (or slow) according to the tempo of the music. Follow the shape of the tune, or make larger movements when the music gets louder.

Later, children can go inside the Music House where several flashlights have been placed, and where a tape recording of music is playing. Children are free to use flashlights to conduct music on the walls of the music house in their own way during free play time.

The light shows children create will allow them to move to, as well as visually depict, the shape of the tune, the tempo and rhythms, or the dynamics of what they hear. Additionally, the environment provides a quiet place for children who need to temporarily withdraw from possible over-stimulation.

BUILDING THE MUSIC HOUSE

BUILDING MATERIALS
- High Table
- Dark sheets
- Children's art work to hang on the sheets (optional)

ASSEMBLY

1. Assembly of the Music House is simple and quick. Place dark sheets over a sturdy, high table.

2. Decorate the outside of the Music House with children's art, if desired.

3. Inside, place several small flashlights and a tape recording of music such as Saint Saens' "The Swan" from *Carnival of the Animals*, and/or Haydn's *Symphony No. 94*, second movement. Children use flashlights to conduct music on the walls of the Music House.

4. For variety, you may wish to place your Music House in a theme setting. Ours was displayed during October, so we decorated with the children's orange and black art work and called it the Surprise House. It was part of our *Pumpkin Playground*, which included six music play centers for children. Other favorites included a dress-up corner with multi-colored scarves and a tape of musical excerpts for dancing, and a bevy of unusual instruments sitting on a blanket. Just think what you could devise around other themes meaningful to children's lives, like "winter," animals," or "spring"! Maybe a Rainy Day Recess? A March Musicale? A Musical Zoo?

Going to the Ocean

APPROPRIATE AGES: 2-8 years

PREKINDERGARTEN MUSIC EDUCATION STANDARDS EXPLORED

Children will

- Use their voices expressively as they speak, chant, and sing
- Sing a variety of simple songs
- Experiment with a variety of instruments
- Improvise song to accompany their play activities
- Respond through movement to music of various tempos, meters, dynamics, modes, genres, and styles to express what they hear and feel in works of music
- Participate freely in music activities
- Sing, move, or verbalize to demonstrate awareness of elements of music and changes in tempo
- Demonstrate awareness of music as part of daily life

WHY THIS ENVIRONMENT?

Children are delighted by a place where they can go to play, dance, sing, and improvise. This environment invites and leads the children to explore sounds. It is flexible so that each day it can be changed to encourage new creative play.

CREATED BY

Mary Ann Hall, founder and director of "Music for Children," 19 Ellery Lane, Westport CT 06880, 1-800-633-0078

The ocean theme encourages children to make music as they pretend to live and play near and in the ocean. Beach buckets carry percussion instruments. Swimming in the ocean might invite children to turn on some swimming music if a tape recorder and tape are nearby.

Ocean drums, bowls of shells, puppets, scarves, ribbons, bubbles, and books all invite musical play that says "Here I am! Play with me!" Teacher-guided activities are added to the children's play to increase their musical skills and awareness.

The flexibility of this environment encourages children to participate in all of the standards when things in the environment are changed.

PLAY MATERIALS
- Cardboard boxes for the ocean box scene
- Ten three-dimensional felt fish
- Round ocean cloth
- Songs: "We're Floating Down the River" and "One in the Middle"

THE PLAY

Sit around a large round ocean cloth cut from a king-size sheet. Put one little felt fish in the middle.

Remind the children:
> *Don't go under the cloth.*
> *Don't go over the cloth.*
> *Sit around the cloth.*

2: Going to the Ocean

Invite the children to hold onto the edge of the cloth and wave it up and down in a smooth motion, "floating the fish" as they sing "Floating Down the River." Invite children to move the cloth in a gentle waving motion to let the fish ride the waves.

We're float-ing down the riv-er___ We're float-ing down be-low___ We're float-ing down the ri-ver___ On the O-hi-o.

When the song has ended, shake the cloth vigorously to jump the fish and sing "One in the middle and you jump, Josie."

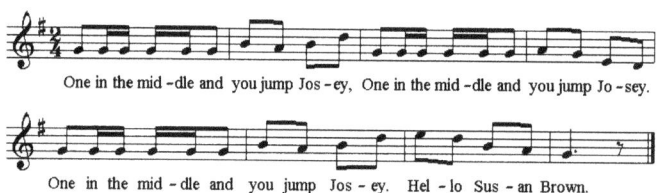

One in the mid-dle and you jump Jos-ey, One in the mid-dle and you jump Jo-sey. One in the mid-dle and you jump Jos-ey. Hel-lo Sus-an Brown.

Alternate the legato floating fish and the staccato jumping fish while singing the songs.

Continue alternating the songs, but add another fish each time until there are 10 fish. ("Ten in the middle and you jump, Josie.")

Place the cloth ocean and the fish in your music play center. Watch the children play on their own. Until they know the song well, sing with them to support their play. Or record your voice singing the song so the children can play a tape to help them sing. What you do and how you do it depends on the age, interests, and needs of your children.

Here are a few other songs that work well when "Going to the Ocean."

"All the Fish Are Swimming in the Water" *traditional*

"The Yellow Submarine" *The Beatles*

"Goin' to the Ocean" *Mary Ann Hall*

"Michael Row the Boat Ashore" *African American traditional*

"Row, Row, Row Your Boat" *traditional*

"Dance with Your Daddy" *traditional*

BUILDING GOING TO THE OCEAN

BUILDING MATERIALS

- Cardboard boxes of varying sizes
- Brushes
- Felt for fish
- Polyester fiberfill stuffing
- Clear packaging tape
- Tempera paints of various colors
- Sponges
- King-size sheet
- Needle and thread

ASSEMBLY

1. Find or purchase different sized boxes. We used four 10- by 10- by 40-inch boxes, four 20-inch square boxes, and one 25- by 25- by 29-inch box.

2. Discuss with children the idea of creating a "box scene" about the ocean. Build enthusiasm about ocean life. Explore colors that might be seen in the ocean, etc.

3. Set up paint, brushes, markers, and sponges and allow children to paint the boxes with background colors.

4. When the boxes are dry, paint designs, shapes, fish, seaweed, etc. on the boxes.

5. Tape boxes together to create cubes, rectangles, and squares.

6. Arrange the boxes in a corner and add instruments, ribbons, scarves, puppets, songs, books, tape player shells, clothes, etc.

2: Going to the Ocean

MAKING THE FISH

Cut fish from felt and hand stitch around, leaving a small opening to add stuffing. Then sew opening closed. We painted quarter notes on our fish.

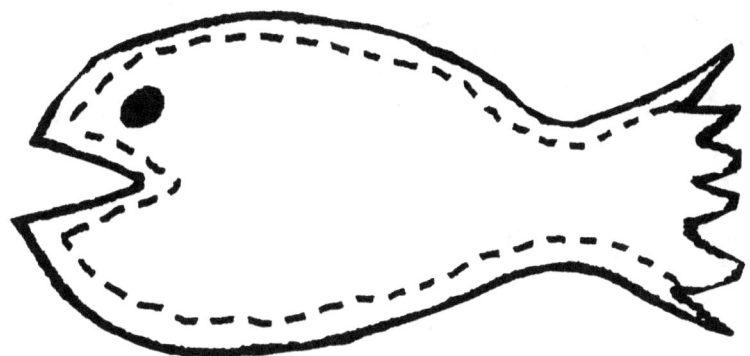

The Music House

APPROPRIATE AGES: 3-5 years

EARLY CHILDHOOD MUSIC EDUCATION STANDARDS EXPLORED

Children can be encouraged to explore all of the standards at different times, depending on the materials set in the environment, and the teacher's lessons.

WHY THIS ENVIRONMENT?

Young children need places where they can go to play and create. This environment provides such a space and is easy to make, inexpensive, and versatile. Furthermore, the children can help create the environment themselves, thus having ownership of the space and the feeling of having accomplished a wonderful play area.

Parents, other teachers, and college students could also be invited to contribute to the environment, making it a truly collaborative effort.

This environment is portable and flexible enough to allow music exploration that meets all of the prekindergarten music education standards while at the same time allowing integration with other areas of the child's life.

CREATED BY

Cecilia Riddell, Music Educator, 526 Michigan Blvd., Pasadena, CA 91107, 626-356-7422
criddell@sprintmail.com

3: Music on a Shoestring

PLAY MATERIALS
- Cardboard panels
- Homemade instruments
  — Buttons or bells strung on shoe laces
  — Frame drum made from a wooden frame wrapped with clear packaging tape. Shoe lace handle
  — Paint stick rhythm paddles
  — Dowel mallets with heads made from wooden beads, cat toy balls, super balls, tennis balls

Props
- Rhythm tapping page with drawings of shoes as rhythms
- Easel and marking pens for "drawing music"
- Shoe boxes filled with interesting shoes, rhythm instruments, books, pictures, tapes, puppets, etc.
- Cassette player and headphones
- Soft pillow for comfortable listening

THE PLAY

The Music on a Shoestring panels provide a backdrop for many kinds of musical play. Some days you can put boxes of instruments in front of the panels ready for creative play.

The pockets on the panels could have cassettes or cds for playing recorded music, and they could contain markers and staff paper for children to write their own music.

Keep a tape recorder nearby for playing music or for recording the children's own singing.

The panels can provide a backdrop for a "dance-movie" set where dress-up clothes are hanging, ready for actors to wear.

The music panels will stimulate musical behaviors and the teacher is always nearby to guide the play or suggest further exploration. Treat the environment as one big prop for whatever you can relate to it.

AN INTEGRATED LESSON

We explored music in relation to shoes, which led to exploration about shoe laces, walking, dancing, running, visiting places, and shoes from other places.

The children were involved in helping make the music panels and we even used shoes in the making. We used shoe laces, for example, to tie the music panels together and shoe boxes for storing things.

Introduce the Topic

During circle time, introduce the topic in front of the music panels and use materials from the panels to explore musical examples and behaviors. Then allow children to explore freely.

Be sure to show playing techniques for all music objects so that nothing is likely to be treated carelessly and provide rules for using equipment such as the cassette player. Use individual headphones for listening to music.

Be Flexible

Consider changing the order of the panels, so that something new is highlighted each day. Show how parts of the panels and puppet stage come apart and fit together again.

Show how two friends can play in the environment together. Show how a shoebox display can be taken apart to reveal musical games, cassettes, instruments, and other treasures.

Ask the children to help invent a system for drawing clues on the outside of each container, so that objects will be put carefully away.

Create Locomotor Pathways

Use the panels not just to support objects, but to create pathways. For example, march around the structure when it is placed in a circle, or zig-zag around if the structure is placed in a zig-zag shape. Sometimes set it up as a rectangle with a doorway.

Integrate With Other Arts

Collect songs, poems, and stories about shoes to share with the children and take advantage of beautiful illustrations and paintings of shoes. Ask the children to draw and paint pictures of themselves dancing in their favorite shoes (or doing other activities—putting out a fire in a fireman's shoes, fishing in fishing shoes, etc.). Provide scarves to encourage children to dance to their favorite music. Use shoes for going places—other cultures, other landscapes, and other parts of your school or city. Find traveling music and music that represents other places and other people. Help children develop cognitive skills by classifying the musical instruments into categories such as woods, metals, shakers, etc. The environment itself will encourage creative thinking, and careful supervision will help them develop cooperative behaviors.

Keep A Record

Video the children before, during, and after their experience in the environment, to serve as a documentary of their adventure. Interview children and write their conversations down in a journal.

BUILDING MUSIC ON A SHOESTRING

BUILDING MATERIALS

- Cardboard—preferably clean packing boxes from a moving company or furniture store
- Knife and scissors
- Wood glue
- Paint sticks, lots of them
- Sandpaper
- Hammer and nails
- Clear packaging tape
- Portable drill
- Sewing machine
- Pieces of felt
- Shiny fabric for curtains
- Fabric to drape over cardboard sections
- Shoe laces—lots of them, too
- Shoe boxes

ASSEMBLY

1. Open up boxes into panels. Cut one side to connect with the next box. Poke holes along sides of connecting panels and attach with shoe laces at top and bottom.

2. Lay the cardboard on the floor and fold back a few bottom panels where there are natural creases. Glue these back to the other side, place weight on the cardboard and allow to dry, then glue on paint sticks for reinforcement and support as needed.

3. Fold up a few bottom panels and score them to make pockets. Reinforce with a paint stick on inside at the bottom. Poke or drill holes to tie up the sides with shoe laces to complete the pockets.

4. Glue felt fabric to one cardboard panel to create a felt board.

5. Add paint sticks in a variety of designs. For example, create a picket fence where small items such as shoes and musical instruments can be hung. Consider creating a 5-line staff.

6. Hang fabric over one or two panels as needed for display. Apply velcro if needed.
7. Make pockets to hold light-weight cards or laminated pieces of paper.
8. Create a puppet stage from boxes and cardboard tubes (see illustration). Drill holes through the tubes to attach rods and stage. Cover the stage loosely with shiny fabric. Prop up a curtain rod by threading a thin dowel through holes in the tubes. Attach tubes to the box below with shoe laces. Use fabric bolts for stage. Attach more shiny material to make curtains.

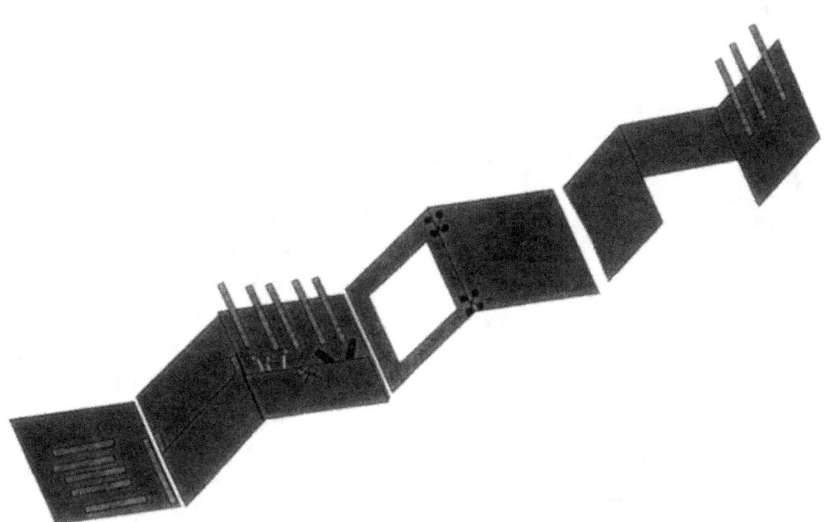

Hickory Dickory Dock

APPROPRIATE AGES: 3-5 years

PREKINDERGARTEN MUSIC EDUCATION STANDARDS EXPLORED

Children will

- Use their voices expressively as they speak, chant, and sing
- Play simple melodies and accompaniments on instruments
- Sing a variety of songs
- Experiment with a variety of instruments
- Improvise instrumental accompaniments
- Play instruments to demonstrate awareness of the elements of music

WHY THIS ENVIRONMENT?

Children enjoy manipulating puzzles and other materials. This environment builds on typical young child behaviors while encouraging musical exploration.

CREATED BY

Barbara Andress, Retired Professor of Music Education, Arizona State University School of Music, Phoenix, AZ

4: Hickory Dickory Dock

PLAY MATERIALS
- Grandfather clock with attached xylophone and wood blocks
- Mallet with heads on both ends of stick

THE PLAY

Many clock/mouse related songs exist in traditional children's song literature. Typically, the teacher plays with the child the first time, demonstrating and incorporating the child's ideas. Later, the child returns to the environment for many repeated self-directed experiences.

The three songs featured in this section are readily played with the grandfather clock. Instructions for making the clock start on page 19.

HICKORY DICKORY DOCK

Set the clock hands at one o'clock then chant:

Hickory, dickory dock (Tap tick-tock sounds alternating between two wood blocks)

The mouse ran up the clock (play xylophone going up)

The clock struck one (strike the "G" bell)

The mouse ran down (play xylophone going down)

Hickory dickory dock (more tick-tock sounds)

Repeat the rhyme and change the hour.

The clock struck 2   The clock struck 3   The clock struck 4   The clock struck 5

THREE BLIND MICE

Insert the wooden mouse dowels in the holes beside the xylophone pitches E-D-C.

Sing the song while playing the indicated pitches. Beginning song pitch is E.

Three (E) blind (D) mice (C) (repeat)

See how they run (mallet up and down on the xylophone—repeat)

They all ran after the farmer's wife (fast up & down on the xylophone)

She cut off their tails with the carving knife (strike wood block)

*Did you ever see such a sight in your life as
Three (E) blind (D) mice (C)*

PIEP, PIEP LITTLE MOUSE

(found in *The Music Book 1*, Holt Rinehart & Winston, Inc., p. 144)
Sing or chant the words to this song while searching for the little mouse. Find the little mouse in the covered hole.

Piep, piep, little mouse

Do not leave your little house.

All the other little mice

Stay inside where it's so nice.

Piep, piep, little mouse

Do not leave your little house.

BUILDING THE GRANDFATHER CLOCK

BUILDING MATERIALS

- Scroll saw or jig saw for cutting wood or
- Scissors for cutting cardboard
- Drill for making holes in wood
- Wood glue
- Screws, screwdriver
- Pattern for grandfather clock (see diagram)
- Refrigerator magnet mice
- 3 dowels, approximately 3 inches long
- One 3" circle of sheet metal

- Xylophone with accurate pitch and quality sound*
- 2 wood blocks*

*the xylophone and wood blocks used for this play are from Peripole Bergerault, Inc. 1-800-443-3592

– xylophone octave bells w/mallet. PB 2308 approx. $30.00

– Clave Tone Block—high sound. PB 5201 approx. $3.00

– Chino Tone Block—medium sound. PB5202 approx. $4.00

HOW TO CREATE THE CLOCK

You can make the grandfather clock in one of three ways:

1. Cut all the parts out of wood or cardboard according to the pattern in the illustration.

or

2. Purchase the wood parts from a craft store and assemble. For the clock face you will need the following:
   - 10-inch round or oval wooden plaque
   - 1-inch numbers from 1 to 12
   - wooden or cardboard clock hands

or

3. Buy a clock face from a teaching supply company

ASSEMBLY

Attach heavy pieces with screws and light pieces with glue, as indicated in the sketch.

Drill three holes next to the xylophone as illustrated and place three short dowels to fit the holes.

Drill a larger hole at the bottom of the clock and screw the sheet metal circle over the hole (using a single screw at the top of the circle) to provide a hiding place for a little mouse. Make the screw loose enough that the sheet metal circle can pivot open and shut.

Glue or screw little mice onto the ends of the dowels. Refrigerator magnets are one source for sturdy little mice. Pull off the magnets and glue the mice to various parts of the clock.

Mice Plugs (A)

PATTERN

Use the pattern in the illustration to construct the grandfather clock. Cut the clock from wood or cardboard according to the dimensions indicated.

4: Hickory Dickory Dock

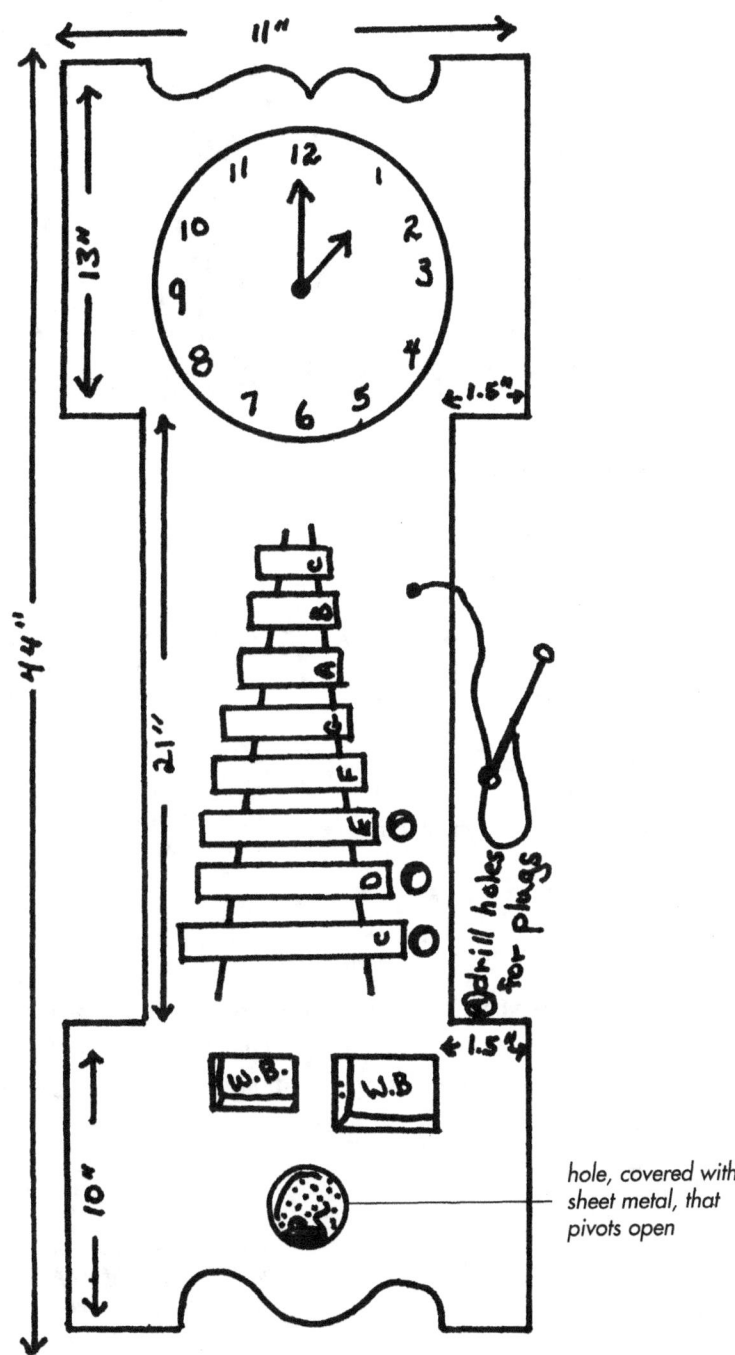

PVC Pipe Playstage

APPROPRIATE AGES: 2-5 years

PREKINDERGARTEN MUSIC EDUCATION STANDARDS EXPLORED

Children will

- Use their voices expressively as they speak, chant, and sing
- Experiment with a variety of instruments and other sound sources
- Improvise songs to accompany their play activities
- Create short pieces of music using voices
- Respond through movement to music of various tempos, meters, dynamics, modes, genres, and styles to express what they hear and feel in works of music
- Participate freely in music activities
- Demonstrate an awareness of music as a part of daily life

WHY THIS ENVIRONMENT?

Children can often be found making little spaces for their play. They may place blankets over chairs, move small furniture around, or make a stage by standing behind a tipped-over chair.

CREATED BY

Susan Kujawski, Music Educator, 870 Villa Nueva Drive, Litchfield Park AZ 85340, 623-935-5195, email: LPPARADOX@aol.com

5: PVC Pipe Playstage

Once a space is defined, all kinds of activities go on as the children create in their imaginative environment. Modeled after what children do, this Playstage creates a space for creative play, encouraging music exploration.

PLAY MATERIALS
- The Playstage
- Play Instruments—Choose a variety of materials for the Stage space:
  - Play microphone
  - Play guitar
  - Tape player with recorded music
  - Scarves or other movement manipulatives
  - Unpitched percussion instruments
  - Small xylophones or glockenspiels

THE PLAY

The PVC Pipe Playstage is intended for open-ended exploration of musical ideas and activities. It can become the music place in the room.

Materials provided for children can and should change to allow children to explore musical expression. A small guitar might be placed in the environment for pretending to be a rock star, or a tape player with prerecorded music for movement might be placed in the center with movement manipulatives placed nearby.

Small percussion instruments might be added for musical exploration.

BUILDING THE PVC PIPE PLAYSTAGE

BUILDING MATERIALS

- 8 3/4-inch slip thread T-connectors (3-pronged connectors with female thread at top) *[See illustration part a]*
- 8 3/4-inch PVC male screw adapters *[See illustration part b]*
- 12 3-foot lengths of 3/4-inch PVC pipe *[See illustration part c]*
- 5.5 yards of fabric for curtains
- Sewing machine or fabric glue for curtains
- Small hacksaw if PVC lengths are not precut

ASSEMBLY

1. Use the T-connectors (a) to attach the four lengths of pipe for the bottom.
2. Use the screw adapters (b) to form the holes for the vertical pieces of pipe.
3. Insert the four vertical pieces of PVC pipe (c).
4. Attach the screw adapters (b) to the tops of each vertical piece.
5. Attach four remaining T-connectors (a) to the screw-in plugs.
6. Do not connect top until curtains have been added.

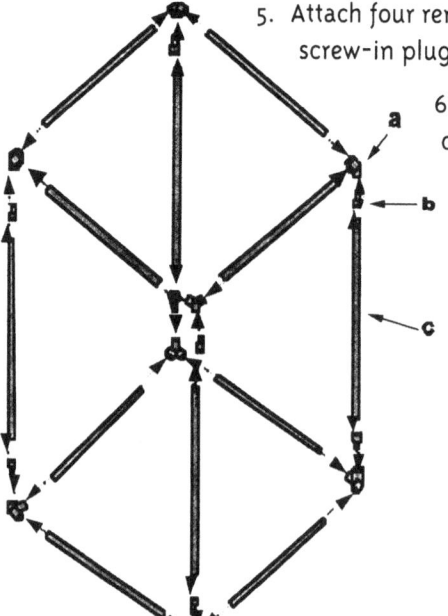

Making the Curtains

1. Cut four panels up to 48 inches long and 45 inches wide—if these are cut with pinking shears they will not have to be hemmed. *Fray Ban* can be used to keep the edges from fraying.

2. Create a casing for the PVC pipe by turning over the top edge 3 inches and sewing or glueing the seam.

3. Cut one panel in half vertically to form the split for the stage curtain.

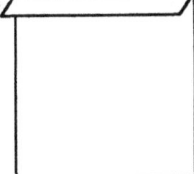

3-inch hem

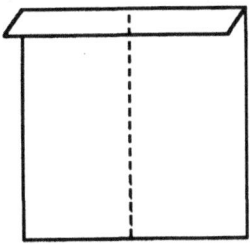

Cut in half for stage curtain

Finishing the Playstage

1. Thread the remaining four pieces of PVC pipe (c) through the casing in the curtains.

2. Attach curtain on pipe to the T-connectors (a) to form the top of the stage.

Tons of Drums

APPROPRIATE AGES: 2-8 years

PREKINDERGARTEN MUSIC EDUCATION STANDARDS EXPLORED

Children will

- Experiment with a variety of instruments and other sound sources
- Play simple melodies and accompaniments on instruments
- Improvise instrumental accompaniments to songs, recorded selections, stories, and poems
- Create short pieces of music, using voices, instruments, and other sound sources
- Invent and use original graphic or symbolic systems to represent vocal and instrumental sounds and musical ideas
- Identify a wide variety of sounds
- Participate freely in music activities

WHY THIS ENVIRONMENT?

Children love to make sounds on just about anything, and drums seem to be a favorite. Building on this natural love for beating drums, the tones of drums can be used to lead children into patterned rhythms, composition, and other expressive music making.

CREATED BY

Mark E. Turner, Asst. Professor of Music, Dept. of Music, Stephen F. Austin State University, email: meturner@sfasu.edu

6: Tons of Drums

PLAY MATERIALS
- At least one set of drums (we use three sets)
- At least two mallets for every drum set

Optional:
- A drawing easel
- Colored shapes or cubes
- Colored pens

THE PLAY

Children will probably not have to be instructed on how to use the drums. Allow them to explore freely and often.

Once the novelty of the drums wears off and the children have exhausted their ideas for sound exploration, renew their interest by helping them discover new sound possibilities.

Consider adding a drawing easel for each set of drums to encourage children to create their own compositions. Draw a pattern of shapes using different colored markers. Have children play the colors that correspond with the drum heads. Before long, your children will create their own music for you and for others.

Another idea is to get a shadow box and use it to hold brightly colored counter manipulatives. Demonstrate how to create musical patterns by making a pattern of colored counters and then encouraging children to play the patterns on the drum by matching the colored drum heads.

Remember, the colors of the counters should correspond to the colors used on the drums.

BUILDING TONS OF DRUMS

BUILDING MATERIALS

- 21 5-gallon buckets

  These can be collected from a variety of sources. Cleaning solutions and floor wax used in schools come in 5-gallon buckets that get thrown away. Or visit a nearby swimming pool supply company and ask for buckets they plan to throw away. Rinse all buckets thoroughly.

- "PlastiDip!"

  Located in the adhesives section of most home improvement stores. It comes in a tall yellow can that looks similar to a can of tennis balls.

- 1/2-inch diameter PVC pipe, cut into 1-inch pieces

  Use scraps or purchase at any home improvement center.

- 18 3/8-inch nuts and bolts, 2-inch length
- 36 washers
- Wood Screws
- Spray paint, at least five different colors
- Tennis balls

  Used, "dead" balls work great and might be donated by a tennis club.

- 1-inch diameter dowel cut into 18-inch lengths
- Washers and 1 1/2-inch wood screws
- Electric drill
- Hacksaw
- Crescent wrenches or socket set
- Screw driver
- Hot glue gun
- Permanent marker

ASSEMBLY

1. Rinse all buckets thoroughly and remove wire handles.

2. Set aside six buckets. These will be the "heads" of the drums.

3. Cut the remaining buckets in half with the hacksaw, as shown in the first figure. Throw away the bottoms. Keep the half that had the handle connected to it (referred to as the collar).

   These collars will be stacked to make drums of different sizes.

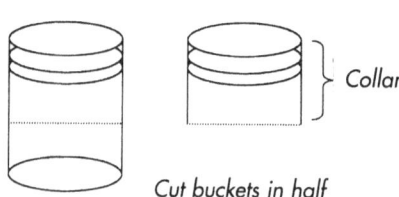

Cut buckets in half

6: Tons of Drums

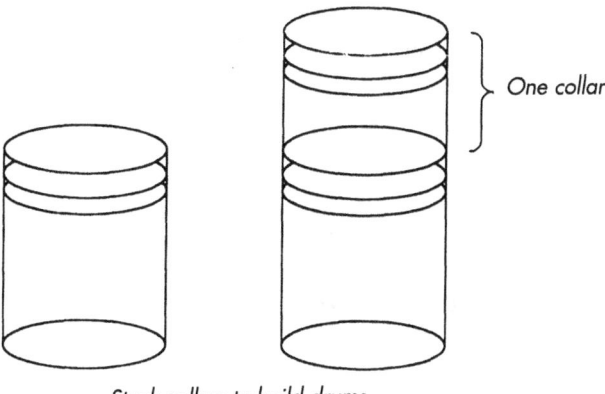

Stack collars to build drums

One collar

4. Get the six buckets you set aside. Five of these will have a bucket collar added. Adding an additional collar to each bucket will change the pitch of that drum. Take the collars out as a "set" and with the wood screws, attach the collars to one another so they will not fall apart.

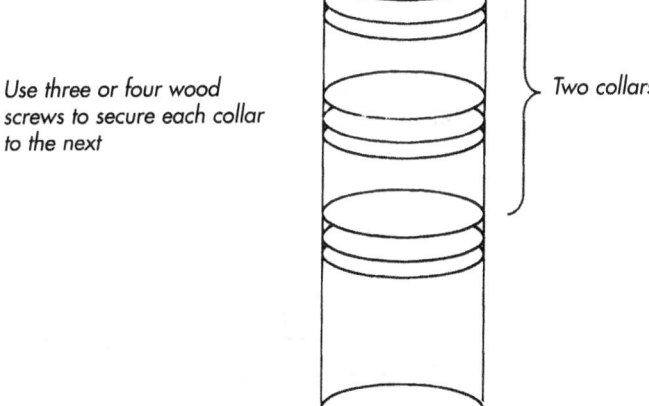

Use three or four wood screws to secure each collar to the next

Two collars

5. Take the six buckets that remain and arrange them to make a triangle.

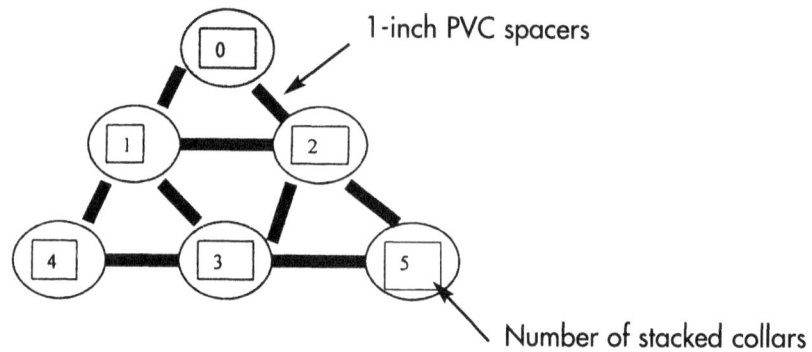

6. With the 3/8-inch drill, drill a hole into the side of one of the buckets about 2 inches from the bottom. Using the first hole as a guide, use a permanent marker to mark a similar spot on another bucket. Drill that hole.

7. Place a 3/8-inch bolt with washers on both ends into the holes to connect the buckets. Be sure to use the 1-inch long PVC pipe as a spacer between the two buckets. You should have, in order:

   a. a bolt
   b. a washer

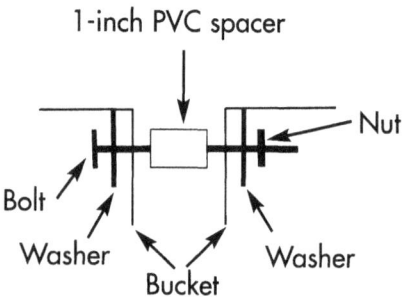

c. a spacer between buckets

  d. a washer, and

  e. a nut

NOTE: Until all buckets are attached to one another, do not tighten with a wrench or socket set.

8. Drill another hole directly above the first, 6 to 9 inches away. Repeat the process noted above. You will need two bolts between every bucket to add stability to the instrument. Continue with this process until all buckets are connected by two bolts.

9. Now, tighten all the bolts snugly.

10. Apply enough hot glue to the threads of each bolt so that the nut will never loosen. If you don't do this, when the drums vibrate, the nuts will loosen and fall off.

11. Lastly, take the collars and place them in the buckets and attach with screws. (See the figure below step 5 for how many collars to have under each drum head.)

12. Apply hot glue to cover all sharp points of the screws.

13. Now you can paint each drum head a different color.

MAKING THE MALLETS

1. Drill a small pilot hole in the end of each dowel, about an inch deep.
2. Cut a small hole in each tennis ball so that it will fit over each dowel.
3. Attach ball to dowel with wood screw. Make certain that you place a small washer on each screw. This will help the ball stay on the dowel.
4. Cover the ball and dowel with "PlastiDip!" This will take several coats. You can jazz up your mallets by using several different colors.

APPROPRIATE AGES: 18 months – 5 years

PREKINDERGARTEN MUSIC EDUCATION STANDARDS EXPLORED

Children will

- Use voices expressively
- Sing a variety of simple songs
- Improvise songs to accompany their play
- Participate freely in music activities
- Demonstrate music as a part of daily life

WHY THIS ENVIRONMENT?

Most singing done with children occurs during gathering time when all sing the same song together. But children need opportunities to sing by themselves both songs they have learned and songs they create as they play. These manipulatives encourage children to sing by themselves.

For those who know the song "Mary Wore A Red Dress," they may begin singing the song as they dress the dolls. Others may make up a song as they play with the dolls.

CREATED BY
Sharla Dance, Music Educator, 7739 234th Place N.E., Redmond, WA 98053

7: Mary Wore a Red Dress

PLAY MATERIALS

- Painted board doll children
- Clothing for each doll

- Book: *Mary Wore Her Red Dress and Henry Wore His Green Sneakers*
  Illustrated by Merle Peek
  ISBN 0-395-90022-0 (optional)

THE PLAY

During gathering time, sing "Mary Wore a Red Dress," substituting each child's name for Mary. Introduce the board dolls Mary and Mark and tell the children that we need to help them get dressed. Select one of Mark's shirts, hold it up and ask children its color. Proceed to sing about Mark's shirt while one child places his shirt on. Continue finding clothes for Mark while singing about each article of clothing. Do the same with Mary.

Make up stories about why Mary and Mark might need to change their clothes. (They spilled jam, fell in the mud, etc.). Change clothes, singing the appropriate color while changing. Consider singing the book *Mary Wore Her Red Dress and Henry Wore His Green Sneakers* to the children.

Place Mary and Mark, their clothing, and the book in a center for the children to use during free play time. Mark the boundaries of the environment in some way (i.e. masking tape circle on the floor, place them on a blanket, etc.)

As the children interact with the board dolls, watch for moments to nonintrusively join in the play. For instance, as a child plays with the girl doll, start to play and sing with the boy doll, or as the child puts on a yellow dress, hum the tune of the song, singing the word yellow.

While the child plays with one of the dolls, you could comment about the stitching lines on the boy's pants and compare it to the stitching lines on the child's clothing, perhaps inserting the child's name and clothing color into the song.

Look for moments to create a personalized song about the board children (sing about their hair, about standing so tall, about being in a preschool) and/or a personalized song about the child interacting with the board dolls. (For example, Becky wears a yellow ribbon, yellow ribbon, yellow ribbon, Becky wears a yellow ribbon as she plays.)

BUILDING MARY AND MARK DOLLS

BUILDING MATERIALS

- 1/4-inch or 1/2-inch plywood cut to 26 by 28 inches
- 100 grit sandpaper
- Carbon or graphite paper
- Paint and brushes
- Two 3-inch hinges and screws
- Felt pieces of different colors
- Velcro pieces, hook side
- Lace
- String or cord for shoe laces
- Patterns of dolls and clothes
- Saw
- Screwdriver
- Sewing machine
- Staple gun and staples

ASSEMBLY

1. Copy the Mary and Mark doll patterns as well as the clothing patterns on an oversize copy machine. Each pattern should fill a paper 36 by 28 inches.

2. Cut two pieces of good quality plywood to measure 36 by 28 inches. Sand all edges. (*Optional:* Cut an oval hand-hole in the top at the same place on both pieces to make the dolls easier to carry around.)

3. Center the enlarged pattern on the wood and transfer all lines of the patterns with carbon paper. One piece of wood is for Mary, the other for Mark.

4. Paint the dolls with colors you think are appropriate.

5. After paint is completely dry, place both pieces face down and top to top. Screw two sets of 3-inch hinges onto each piece of wood, making sure they are aligned so they won't wobble when they are stood up (see diagram). Staple the velcro pieces in place (see dark squares on doll patterns).

6. Cut clothes from colored felt and follow directions on pattern.

7: Mary Wore a Red Dress

7: Mary Wore a Red Dress

7: Mary Wore a Red Dress

MARY AND MARK CLOTHES

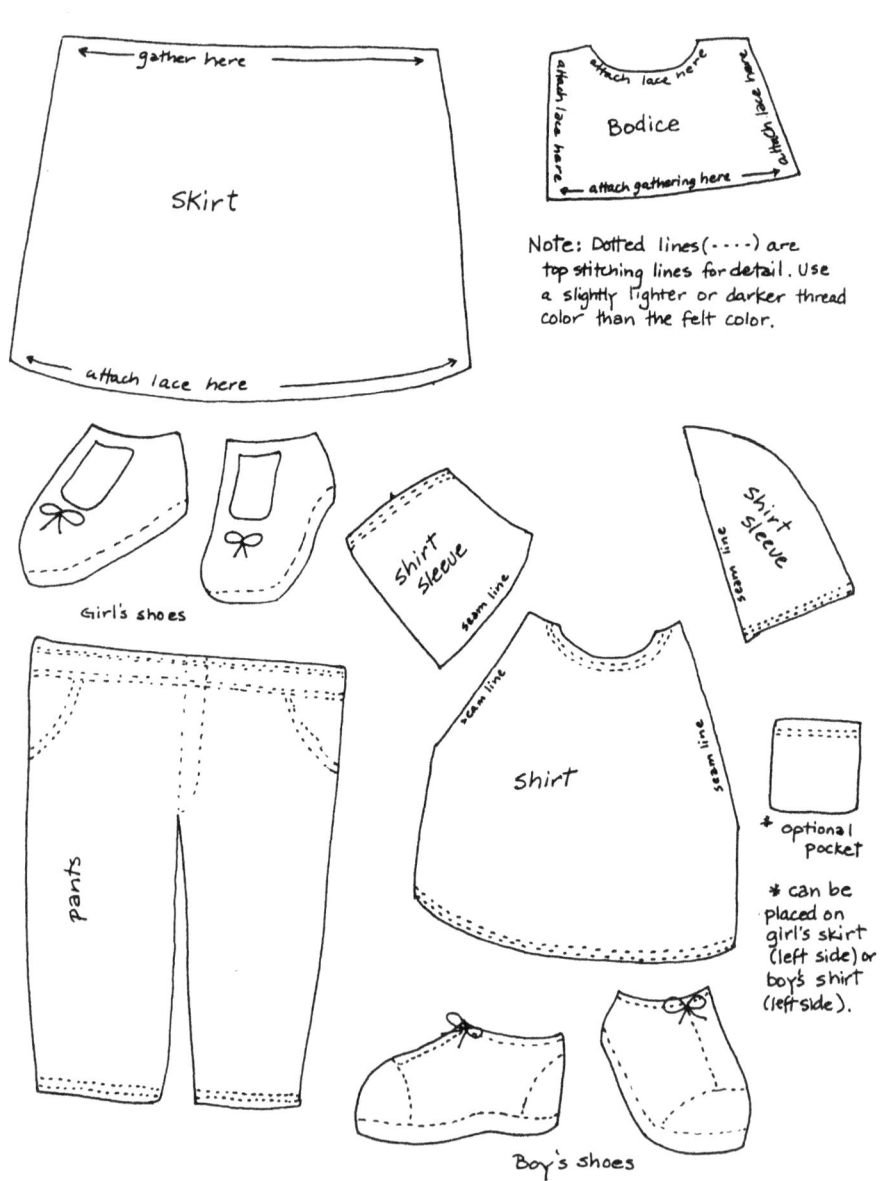

The Music Box

APPROPRIATE AGES: 2-6 years

PREKINDERGARTEN MUSIC EDUCATION STANDARDS EXPLORED

Children will

- Use voices expressively
- Sing a variety of simple songs
- Experiment with a variety of instruments
- Improvise songs to accompany their play
- Use symbolic systems to represent vocal and musical ideas
- Identify the sources of a wide variety of sounds
- Respond through movement to music of various tempos, meters, dynamics, modes, genres, and styles to express what they hear and feel in works of music
- Participate freely in music activities
- Use vocabulary to describe music sounds, instruments, and notation

WHY THIS ENVIRONMENT?

Children enjoy special places where they often let their imaginations run wild. The Music Box is a special music place. It was designed to encourage children to experience a variety of music processes, to build music understanding, and to stimulate creativity. Because so many activities are possible with the Music Box, caregivers should be cautioned not to offer all the possibilities at one time.

CREATED BY

Susan H. Kenney, Brigham Young University School of Music, Provo, Utah 84602
susan_kenney@byu.edu

8: The Music Box

PLAY MATERIALS

- Music Box
- Magnetic notes
- Cardboard instrument pictures with magnetic strip
- Assorted rhythm instruments (2 of each)
- Tape recorder
- Recordings of music
- Scarves, flashlights

THE PLAY

During gathering time, demonstrate for the children how to play with the instrument wall, the magnetic wall, and the window wall. You may wish to introduce one wall one day, and other walls another day.

Instrument Wall

Encourage children to explore freely the instruments in the pockets. When they are ready, they may wish to play the matching game. One child sits on either side of the wall. One child finds an instrument and makes it sound. The child on the other side of the wall listens, then finds the sound that matches. Children then stand and show each other the match. Continue the play as long as children are interested. After the instrument wall has been demonstrated, place it in the environment for free exploration.

Magnetic Wall

Take the notes (page 41) from the pockets and place them on the staff. Notice that the staff has lines and spaces. When the notes are placed on the higher lines/spaces, sing high sounds, on lower lines/spaces, sing low sounds. If notes are placed going up, sing up the scale, etc. When a child places the notes on the staff, "sing" the song they have written. Help build vocabulary by naming the notes as children handle them—quarter note, eighth note, whole note, half note.

Place anything that has a magnetic strip on the other side of the wall. We laminated cardboard instrument cutouts then glued magnetic strips to the back. As children place the instruments on the wall, name the instruments and pretend to play them. What else might be used on this wall?

Make a copy machine enlargement of the note patterns illustrated. Adjust the size to fit the staff drawn on the magnetic wall (page 44). Draw onto 1/2-inch plywood. Cut, sand, and paint. Paste magnetic strips to the back of each note.

Window Wall

Place recordings such as *Carnival of the Animals* of Saint-Saens, *The Four Seasons* by Vivaldi, and/or other recordings in the pockets of the wall. Place scarves or ribbons in the large pocket so children can dance to the music. Place a child-safe tape recorder on the floor. Encourage children to play the music and listen quietly or move to the music. This wall has a window to play peek-a-boo through or to sing "I see you." The other side of the wall has a velcro strip across for hanging various song starters. Shown in this display is "I Know an Old Lady" and Window Songs.

"I Know an Old Lady" Song Starter

Sing "I Know an Old Lady" and drop cutouts, puppets, bean bag animals, etc. into the lady's mouth while singing about the object. When all of the animals have been swallowed, lift the lady's apron and unzip to free all of the objects.

8: The Music Box

Window Songs Starter

Use a wooden bluebird, a puppet, or stuffed bird and drop it through each window while singing "Bluebird Bluebird through My Window." On the last phrase, the bird drops in the pocket to take a rest. Change the song by using birds of different colors.

Use the same bird and sing "Tideo." Place a bell in the pocket. On the last phrase, "Jingle at the Window," pull the bell from the pocket and play it.

Bluebird

Blue - bird, blue - bird through my win - dow. Blue - bird, blue - bird through my win - dow.

Blue - bird blue - bird through my win - dow. Oh John - ny aren't you tir - ed.

The Night Wall

Place this wall over the top of the box and let it fall down over the opening. The stars face in to create a feeling of night. Place flashlights and tapes with soft music in the pockets of the side wall. Play the music as the child rests under the stars, or dances the flashlight shining on the ceiling.

Tideo

Pass one win - dow, Ti - de - o. Pass two win - dows, Ti - de - o.

Pass three win - dows, Ti - de - o. Jin - gle at the win - dow, Ti - de - o.

Ti - de - o, Ti - de - o, Jin - gle at the win - dow, Ti - de - o.

BUILDING THE MUSIC BOX

BUILDING MATERIALS

- A piece of fabric 6 by 3 feet for each side of the box and enough more to make pockets (fabric store)
- Eight 3/4-inch slip thread T's (three-pronged connectors with female screw top)
- Twelve 3-foot lengths of 3/4-inch PVC pipe
- Eight 3/4-inch PVC male screw adapters
- 18- by 24-inch metal board (sign making store)
- 6 yards velcro strip (fabric store)
- 1/2-inch plywood scrap for cutting out notes (lumber warehouse)
- Band saw or scroll saw for cutting out notes (industrial arts rooms in schools?)
- Magnetic sheet for cutting and placing on back of notes and instruments (sign making store)
- Set of cutouts of instruments of the orchestra (school supply store)

ASSEMBLY

To make the frame, see "Building the PVC Pipe Playhouse."

Each wall of the Music Box uses one piece of fabric 2 by 6 feet. Fabric will be doubled to make the wall, but all work on each piece of fabric must be completed before doubling fabric to complete the wall.

Rhythm Instrument Wall (Yellow—left side)

1. Hem long length of fabric on each long side
2. Cut strips, hem and sew them onto the fabric, making pockets of various sizes to hold a variety of instruments. Sew the same number of pockets on each end of the fabric strip. Make sure pockets on each end are open toward the center.
3. Fold fabric in center and stitch across about 3 inches from center fold to make a casing for the pvc pipe.

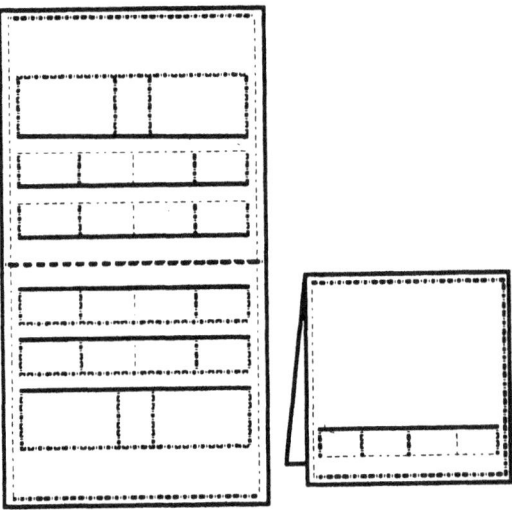

Rhythm Instrument Wall, showing pockets and folded fabric

4. Turn under the ends of the fabric to make a wall that will measure approximately 3 feet. (Make it fit the frame.) Sew the ends together then sew again about 3 inches from first stitching to make a casing for the bottom pvc pipe.
5. Sew side edges together. Do not sew casings closed.
6. Place wall on pvc pipe and prepare to place on Music Box.

Magnetic Wall (Red—right side)

1. Hem length of fabric on each side then mark the center of the fabric.

2. Sew one row of pockets at least 6 inches from the edge of each end of the fabric

3. On one side of the fold, cut out a "window" of fabric 15 by 21 inches. Slit corners in 1-inch diagonals as shown. Fold under 1 inch and hem all sides. Sew on velcro strip on all edges of window, inside.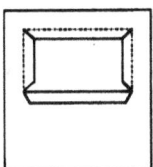

4. Fold fabric in center and stitch across about 3 inches from center fold to make a casing for the pvc pipe.

5. Sew a pocket for the 18- by 24-inch metal magnet-board. (Sew 2 to 3 inches away from the edge of the window.)

6. Turn under the ends of the fabric to make a wall approximately 3 feet high. Sew the ends together then sew again about 3 inches from first stitching to make a casing for the bottom pvc pipe.

7. Sew one side together. Leave the other open for placing the metal board.

8. Draw a staff and G clef on metal board or use black car-striping tape.

9. Place metal board into the wall.

10. Place wall on pvc pipe and prepare to place on Music Box.

Window Wall (Orange—back side)

1. Hem long length of fabric on each side.
2. Cut, hem, and stitch strips across one end of the fabric to make pockets for tapes, CDs, and scarves or ribbons.
3. Sew two strips of velcro (soft side) across the center of the fabric strip.
4. Fold fabric in center and stitch across about 3 inches from center fold to make a casing for the pvc pipe.
5. Turn under the ends of the fabric enough so that from the middle fold to the end is approximately 3 feet. Sew the ends together then sew again about 3 inches from first stitching to make a casing for the bottom pvc pipe.
6. Sew sides together. Do not sew casings closed.
7. To make the window, cut a rectangle of the desired size through both layers. We made ours 7.5 by 8 inches. Then cut in 1-inch corners, fold under, and press. The opening is now 8.5 by 9 inches. Place a piece of clear plastic vinyl (12 inches square) in the opening and stitch along all sides. Panel is now complete. One side is ready for a listening center, the other is ready for singing play additions.

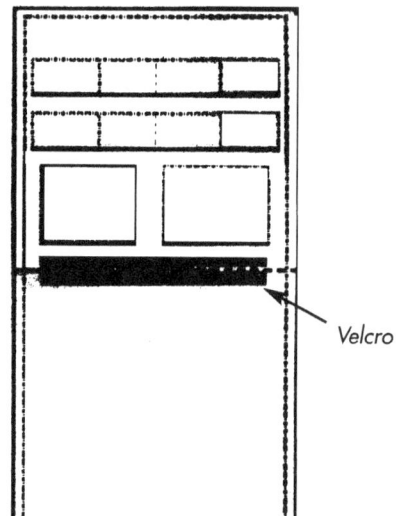
Velcro

"I Know an Old Lady"

1. Cut entire dress (back pattern without the head) from a bright colored fabric. Cut head and applique to dress.

2. Sew a zipper into dress near bottom.

3. Cut hair, eyes, hands, and apron from appropriate colored fabric and applique to dress and head. Leave apron free along sides and bottom in order to get to the zipper. Stitch lines to complete the arms.

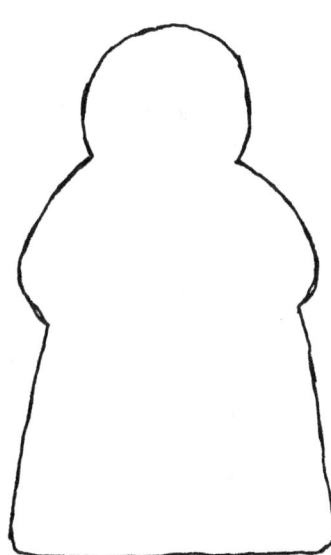

"I Know an Old Lady" patterns. Enlarge on photo copy machine to 31-inch lengths

Window Songs

1. Cut three rectangles from clear vinyl.
2. Cut strips of fabric 3 inches wide to fold over edge of vinyl to make a frame. Stitch in place.
3. Cut a background 18 by 24 inches and hem all four sides. Sew the hook side of velcro onto top. Sew windows and pocket onto background as shown.

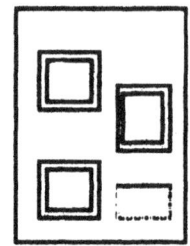

Night Wall (Blue—top and front entrance)

1. Hem on all four sides, then make a casing and sew it onto the center, inside.
2. Sew glow-in-the-dark stars on inside of fabric if you wish.
3. Sew a strip of velcro (hook side) to one end of the wall, inside.

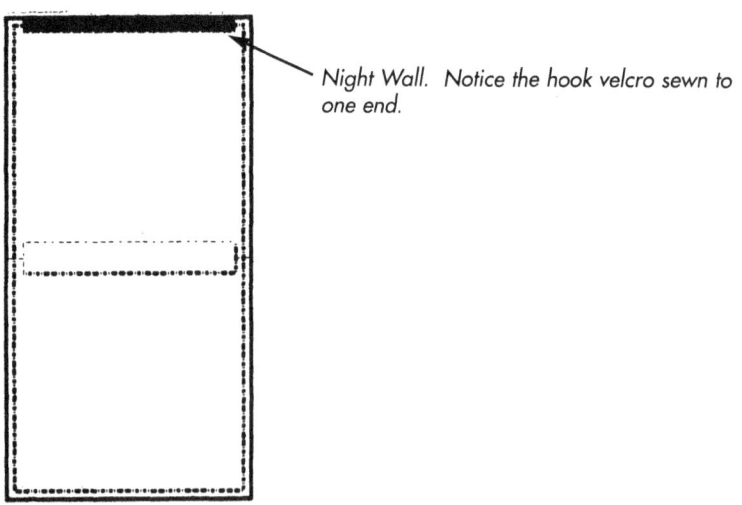

Night Wall. Notice the hook velcro sewn to one end.

What a Wonderful World

APPROPRIATE AGES: 3-8 years

PREKINDERGARTEN MUSIC EDUCATION STANDARDS EXPLORED

Children will

- Sing a variety of songs, alone and with a group, becoming increasingly accurate in rhythm and pitch
- Experiment with a variety of instruments and sound sources
- Play simple melodies and accompaniments on instruments
- Use graphic or symbolic systems to represent vocal and instrumental sounds and ideas
- Identify the sources of a wide variety of sounds
- Participate freely in music activities
- Demonstrate an awareness of music as a part of daily life

WHY THIS ENVIRONMENT?

Singing is an important part of children's lives. Helping them learn sensitive, joyful songs adds to the beauty of their lives and can provide opportunity to learn about other aspects of life. This play environment was developed out of experiences related to the song "What a Wonderful World," and is based on the children's book of the same name.

CREATED BY
Donna Brink Fox, Eastman School of Music, Rochester, New York. 716-274-1544
dbf@mail.rochester.edu

9: What a Wonderful World

This play environment uses the ideas as presented in the *What a Wonderful World* book to invite musical participation. This particular music environment also provides an opportunity to study colors, plants, animals, family life, other cultures, sequencing, and a variety of other non-musical concepts. By looking at the total life experience through music, learning is enhanced and made exciting.

PLAY MATERIALS

- "What a Wonderful World," song by Weiss & Thiele
- *Chicken Soup for Little Souls*. Rhino Entertainment, 1998
- *What a Wonderful World* picture book by Weiss, Thiele, and Bryan. Atheneum Books for Young Readers, 1995
- *Brown Bear, Brown Bear* picture book by Bill Martin, Jr., Holt Rinehart & Winston, 1983

THE PLAY

Focused listening: Introduce the song to the children, noting the specific focus of each verse as illustrated in the *What a Wonderful World* book.

Color classification: While listening to the first verse, identify the colors used. Arrange colored cards as you sing or listen. Create new lyrics using colors and items in the classroom (e.g., "I see shoes of brown—blue jeans, too. . .").

In the play environment encourage children to create their own version of what they see. Use the "My Singing World" box to prompt ideas (see below).

Focused observation: Use the book *Brown Bear* to ask children "what do you see?" Sing the question on sol-mi, encourage children to respond. Use puppets and stuffed animals to prompt singing. Place the book and puppets/stuffed animals in the play environment for children to continue musical questions and answers.

Duration-plant growth: Verse 1 introduces trees and flowers, then says "I see them bloom." Discuss growth and the fact that it takes time. Plant flower seeds (marigolds) and keep track of growth and blossoms on the calendar.

Duration-cycles: Verse 2 develops ideas of day and night. Ask children what things happen at night, in the day. Place the "My Wonderful World Box" in the play environment. Listen to "Oh What a Beautiful Morning" or "Good Morning Starshine" from the *Chicken Soup* album. Use movement to encourage "waking up" actions.

Duration-human growth: Verse 3 explores the idea of babies who cry then grow into families. Develop the theme of "How I've changed since I was a baby." Encourage children to dramatize baby care, including singing to babies to calm them. (Lullabies)

Duration-musical time: Direct movements to match the form of the song; three similar movements on the A sections, changing the movement on the bridge section; A1-A2-B-A3 form.

Space: Design movements that illustrate the spatial differences of below, above, and on the same level.

Use low level movements on verse 1—things that grow in the earth; high level movements on verse 2—things above our heads; and same level movements on verse 3—people and relationships. In the play environment, invite children to create a representation of these levels by placing pictures of objects (or drawing them) at one of these levels.

Seriation: Create picture cards for the lyrics of the song. Order the cards while singing or listening. Design a map for the song.

9: What a Wonderful World

BUILDING "WHAT A WONDERFUL WORLD"

BUILDING MATERIALS

- 4 boxes containing pictures, instruments, scarves, and other items described below

The environment for *Building a Wonderful World* can be made simply by designating a specific space in the room—a blanket on the floor or a bookcase can create a boundary.

You may wish to make a puppet stage, which would require a cardboard box and knife to cut out a window for the stage.

ASSEMBLY

The following items can be used to encourage the play, in addition to those listed at the beginning of this environment description.

- A puppet show stage. This could be made from a large cardboard box with a cut-out square for the presenters to use their puppets or objects (see ideas in Chapter 3, "Music on a Shoestring").
- Blow-up plastic globe of the world
- Four "My World" boxes

BOX #1: MY WONDERFUL WORLD

Include small pictures that illustrate the segments of the lyrics of the song, allow children to listen to the song/recording and match the pictures along the listening map. Include copies of the segments of the lyrics on small placards for use in the puppet show theater. Invite children to draw their own picture for the third verse.

BOX #2: MY INSTRUMENT WORLD

Include one melody instrument (xylophone or glockenspiel) plus 4 or 5 unpitched percussion instruments. Include cards with names of instruments in an envelope for matching. Invite children to accompany their singing and to explore same/different sounds of instruments. One player can go behind the puppet theater and play an instrument for others to identify. Also include pictures of standard musical instruments as performers are invited to the class.

BOX #3: MY SINGING WORLD

Include pictures and word labels for songs from the Chicken Soup album and other "world" songs to prompt singing. Provide puzzle chart for sequencing activities. *Example: He's Got the Whole World in His Hands.*

BOX #4: MY DANCING WORLD

Include scarves and props for movements that allow children to use expressive ideas while listening to "This Pretty Planet" recording. Also use "Zip-A-Dee-Doo-Dah" from the *Chicken Soup* album for movement contrast.

www.ingramcontent.com/pod-product-compliance
Lightning Source LLC
Chambersburg PA
CBHW071934240426
43668CB00038B/1801